CELEBRATE KWANZAA WITH PAPER CRAFTS

Celebrate Holidays with Paper Crafts

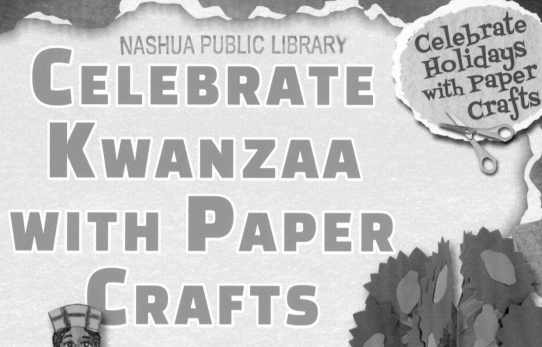

Randel McGee

Enslow Elementary

an imprint of

Enslow Publishers, Inc.

40 Industrial Road
Box 398
Berkeley Heights, NJ 07922
USA

http://www.enslow.com

Dedicated to my parents, Jack and Mable McGee.
They kept my early paper sculptures for decades,
even though some had faded and flopped with age.

This book meets the National Standards for Arts Education.

Enslow Elementary, an imprint of Enslow Publishers, Inc.
Enslow Elementary® is a registered trademark of Enslow Publishers, Inc.

Copyright © 2015 by Randel McGee

Originally published as *Paper Crafts for Kwanzaa* in 2008.

Library of Congress Cataloging-in-Publication Data

McGee, Randel.
  [Paper crafts for Kwanzaa]
  Celebrate Kwanzaa with paper crafts / Randel McGee.
      pages cm. — (Celebrate holidays with paper crafts)
  Audience: Grades K to grade 3.
  "Originally published as Paper crafts for Kwanzaa in 2008."
  Includes bibliographical references and index .
  ISBN 978-0-7660-6370-9 (hardback) — ISBN 978-0-7660-6371-6 (paperback) — ISBN 978-0-7660-6372-3 (EPUB)
— ISBN 978-0-7660-6373-0 (single-user PDF) — ISBN 978-0-7660-6374-7 (multi-user PDF) 1. Kwanzaa decorations—
Juvenile literature. 2. Paper work—Juvenile literature. I. Title.
  TT900.K92M34 2015
  745.594'1612—dc23
                        2014025030

Summary: "Discusses the history of Kwanzaa and how to make eight holiday-themed paper crafts"—Provided by publisher.

Future editions:
Paperback ISBN: 978-0-7660-6371-6   EPUB ISBN: 978-0-7660-6372-3
Single-User PDF ISBN: 978-0-7660-6373-0   Multi-User PDF ISBN: 978-0-7660-6374-7

Printed in the United States of America

102014 Bang Printing, Brainerd, Minn.

10 9 8 7 6 5 4 3 2 1

To Our Readers: We have done our best to make sure all Internet addresses in this book were active and appropriate when we went to press. However, the author and the publisher have no control over and assume no liability for the material available on those Internet sites or on other Web sites they may link to. Any comments or suggestions can be sent by e-mail to comments@ enslow.com or to the address on the back cover.

♻ Enslow Publishers, Inc., is committed to printing our books on recycled paper. The paper in every book contains 10% to 30% post-consumer waste (PCW). The cover board on the outside of each book contains 100% PCW. Our goal is to do our part to help young people and the environment, too!

Illustration Credits: Crafts prepared by Randel McGee and photo on p. 47; craft photography by Nicole diMella/Enslow Publishers, Inc.

Cover Illustration: Craft prepared by Randel McGee; craft photography by Nicole diMella/Enslow Publishers, Inc.

Contents

AUTHOR'S NOTE: Many of the materials used in making these crafts may be found by using recycled paper products. The author uses such recycled items as cereal boxes and similar packaging for light cardboard, manila folders for card stock paper, leftover pieces of wrapping paper, and so forth. This not only reduces the cost of the projects but is also a great way to reuse and recycle paper. Be sure to ask an adult for permission before using any recycled paper products.

The projects in this book were created for this particular holiday. However, I invite readers to be imaginative and find new ways to use the ideas in this book to create different projects of their own. Please feel free to share pictures of your work with me through www.mcgeeproductions.com. Happy crafting!

KWANZAA!

Kwanzaa is a holiday celebrated by people in many countries around the world. It was started in 1966 by Dr. Maulana R. Karenga, a professor of Black Studies at California State University, Long Beach. It is based on harvest celebrations from the people of Africa. *Swahili* is an African language, and it is the language that is used to describe the principles (rules for good behavior), symbols, and actions that go with Kwanzaa. While Kwanzaa has African roots, its principles are ones celebrated by all people.

Nguzo Saba (en-GOO-zoh SAH-bah), Seven Guiding Principles			
Principle	**Pronunciation**	**Translation**	**Meaning**
Umoja	oo-MOH-jah	Unity	Unity of family, race, and community
Kujichagulia	koo-jee-chah-goo-LEE-ah	Self-determination	To take charge of your life and improve it
Ujima	oo-JEE-mah	Helping Others	To work with others so that everyone is secure and successful
Ujamaa	oo-JAH-mah-ah	Community Prosperity	To support the strengths and resources of your community
Nia	NEE-ah	Purpose	To give everyone a sense of direction and an appreciation for their traditions
Kuumba	koo-OOM-bah	Creativity	To make works of beauty and efficiency for the community to enjoy
Imani	ee-MAH-nee	Faith	To believe strongly in your people and your family and that justice and equality will win

Kwanzaa, which means "the first fruits" in Swahili, is a week-long celebration that begins on December 26 and ends January 1. Kwanzaa is not considered a religious holiday, but it is a time to celebrate one's family, achievements, and heritage. It is a time to think about positive values, how to help each other, setting goals, and improving your community. Use your creativity to make the following crafts to help you celebrate Kwanzaa.

The Seven Symbols Of Kwanzaa			
Principle	**Pronunciation**	**Translation**	**Meaning**
Kinara	kee-NAH-rah	Candle Holder	African ancestors
Mkeka	em-KAY-kah	Mat	A foundation or base
Mishumaa Saba	Mee-shoo-MAH-ah SAH-bah	Seven Candles	Seven Kwanzaa principles
Muhindi	Moo-HEEN-dee	Ear of Corn	Each child in the family
Mazao	Mah-ZAH-oh	Crops (basket of fruit and vegetables)	The harvest
Kikombe cha Umoja	kee-KOHM-bay chah oo-MOH-jah	Unity Cup	Unity of the family and community
Zawadi	zah-WAH-dee	Gifts	Shows love of parents for their children and children for their parents

Kinara Pop-up Card

The *kinara* is the candleholder of Kwanzaa. It is decorated with seven candles: three red candles on the left, a black candle in the middle, and three green candles on the right. Black, red, and green are the colors of Kwanzaa. Black stands for the African people, red symbolizes continuing struggle, and green represents the future for the people.

This pop-up kinara and its candles are made from paper, and tissue paper is used for the flames. It can be used as a greeting card, a decoration, or both.

What you will need

- tracing paper
- pencil
- white card stock paper (8 ½ x 11 inches)
- markers or crayons
- scissors
- white glue
- construction paper of any color (8 ½ x 11 inches)
- yellow tissue paper

WHAT TO DO

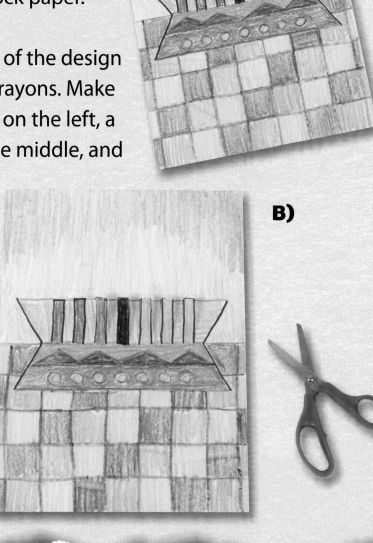

A)

B)

1. Use tracing paper to transfer the pattern from page 38 to the white card stock paper.

2. Color the candles of the design with markers or crayons. Make three red candles on the left, a black candle in the middle, and three green candles on the right. Decorate the kinara and the inside of the card as you wish (See A).

3. Cut the solid lines of the pattern (See B).

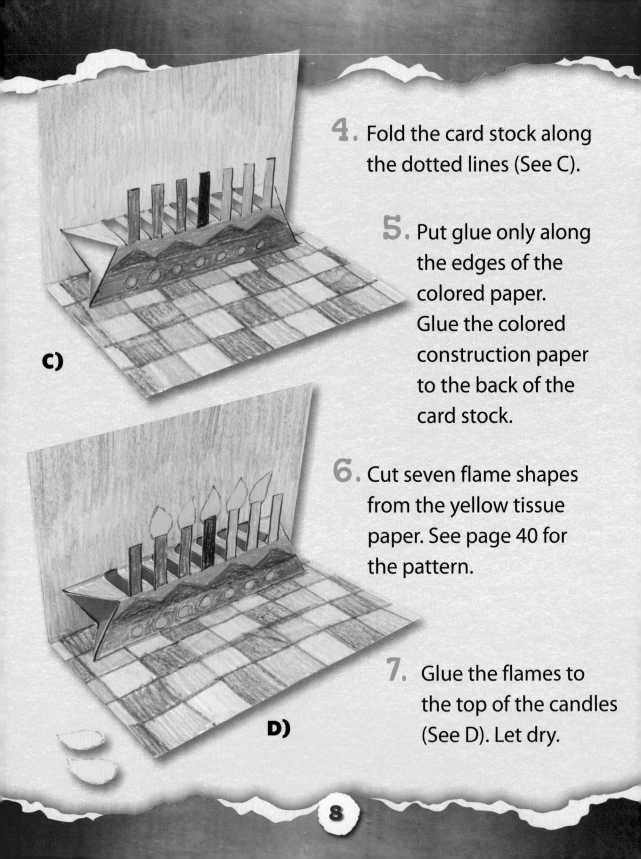

4. Fold the card stock along the dotted lines (See C).

C)

5. Put glue only along the edges of the colored paper. Glue the colored construction paper to the back of the card stock.

6. Cut seven flame shapes from the yellow tissue paper. See page 40 for the pattern.

D)

7. Glue the flames to the top of the candles (See D). Let dry.

8. Write a greeting on the outside or inside of the card.

The Mat (Mkeka)

The *mkeka* is the woven mat that decorates the Kwanzaa table. It is usually woven from straw or other natural fibers. It holds the other symbols of Kwanzaa: the kinara, the seven candles, the unity cup, the ears of corn, the basket of fruits and vegetables, and the useful gifts. Here is a mat that you can weave from paper for your Kwanzaa table.

What You Will Need

- ruler
- pencil
- one sheet of yellow construction paper (12 x 18 inches)
- one sheet of light brown construction paper (12 x 18 inches)
- scissors
- white glue

WHAT TO DO

1. Use a ruler and pencil to draw lines that are 2 inches apart and 18 inches long on the yellow construction paper. Use a ruler and pencil to draw lines that are 2 inches apart and 12 inches long on the light brown construction paper.

2. Cut along the lines on both sheets of paper.

3. Weave all the strips of light brown paper and all the strips of yellow paper together.

4. Glue all loose ends. Let dry.

EAR OF CORN (MUHINDI)

An ear of corn called *muhindi* is placed on the mat for each child that lives in the home. Even if there are no children in a home, an ear of corn is placed on the mkeka to remind everyone that children are the hope for the future. The ear of corn here is made of paper and will stay fresh for a long time.

WHAT YOU WILL NEED

- toilet tissue tube
- white glue
- scissors
- yellow tissue paper (7 x 9 inches)
- yarn (yellow or tan)
- markers or crayons (optional)
- green crepe paper
- clear tape

WHAT TO DO

A)

1. Lightly coat the toilet tissue tube with glue and wrap the yellow tissue around the tube. You may need to cut the tissue paper to about 7 inches by 9 inches, and it should extend beyond the tube about 2 inches on both ends. Glue the yellow tissue along the open seam (See A). Let dry.

2. Place four pieces of yarn about 4 inches long in one end of the tissue-wrapped tube. Put a drop of glue on the inside of the tissue paper and twist it closed around the yarn (See B). This is the ear of corn. If you wish, use a marker or crayon to draw lines on the tube to look like the rows of corn kernels.

B)

3. Draw and cut four corn leaves from the green crepe paper. See page 38 for the pattern.

C)

4. Glue three corn leaves along the length of the ear of corn so that the points are even with the top of the corn where the yarn is (See C). Overlap the leaves slightly. The bottom of the leaves should go about 4 inches below the ear of corn (See D).

D)

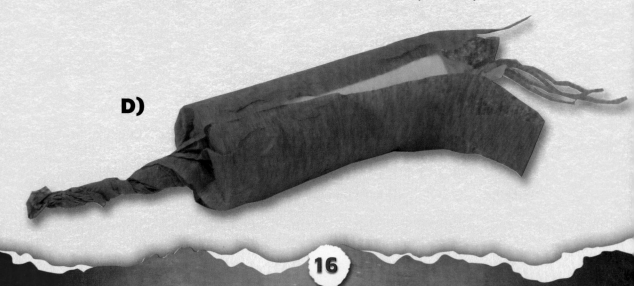

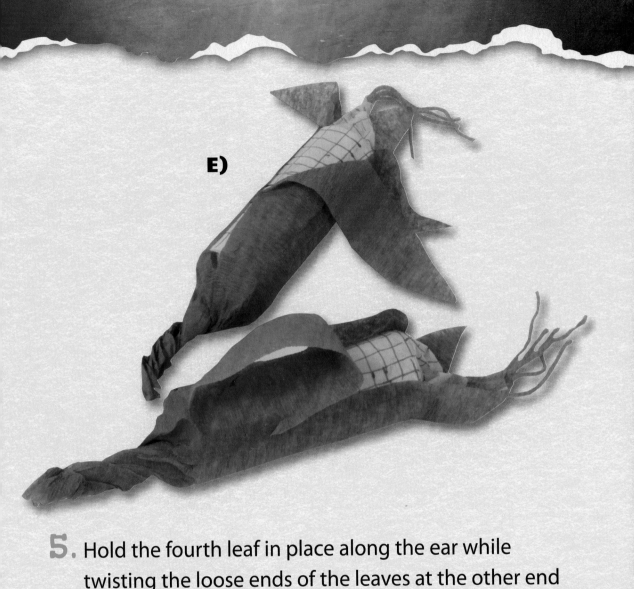

5. Hold the fourth leaf in place along the ear while twisting the loose ends of the leaves at the other end to form the stem. Glue the fourth leaf in place near the bottom of the ear of corn.

6. Wrap the end of the stem with clear tape to secure it (See E).

Standing Kwanzaa Figures

Umoja means "unity." When people help each other, they can accomplish more than if they work only by themselves. These figures, dressed in traditional African clothes, stand together and hold hands as a symbol of their pledge to help one another.

What You Will Need

- tracing paper
- pencil
- white poster board
- markers or crayons
- scissors
- construction paper of any color (optional)
- pieces of cloth (optional)

WHAT TO DO

1. Use tracing paper and a pencil to transfer the patterns from page 41 to the poster board.

2. Color the faces and clothes of the figure. If you wish, use pieces of construction paper or cloth to decorate your figure (See A). Make at least four figures.

3. Cut out the figure along the solid lines. Cut the line on each hand to make a slit (See B).

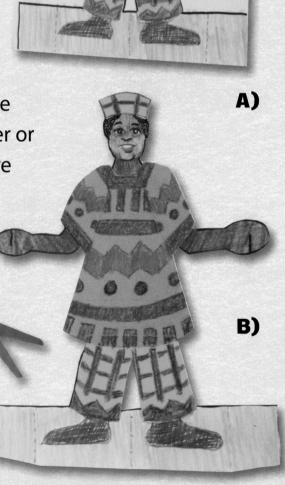

A)

B)

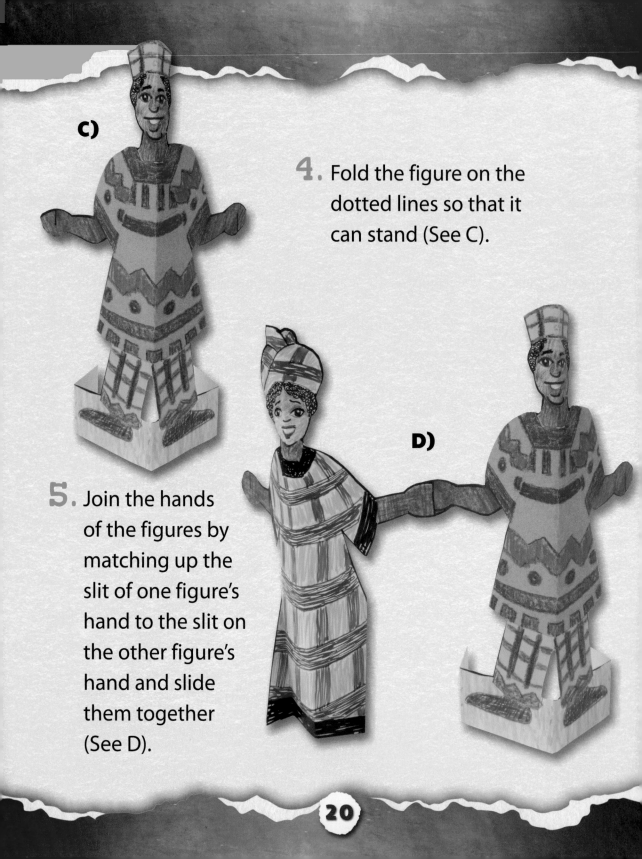

C)

4. Fold the figure on the dotted lines so that it can stand (See C).

D)

5. Join the hands of the figures by matching up the slit of one figure's hand to the slit on the other figure's hand and slide them together (See D).

6. Stand the figures together on a table or countertop.

STANDING FRUIT TREE

Kwanzaa means "the first fruits." It is a celebration of a bountiful harvest when all the fruits and vegetables are ripe and ready to eat. Fruits and vegetables are the crops, or *mazao*. They are placed in a basket and set on the Kwanzaa table. This tree decoration is a symbol of that harvest. There are patterns for three different fruits to choose from to decorate this tree, or you can place all sorts of fruits on it to represent a bountiful crop.

WHAT YOU WILL NEED

- tracing paper
- pencil
- white poster board
- brown poster paint
- paintbrush
- crayons or markers (optional)
- scissors
- green construction paper
- construction paper in any color
- white glue
- clear tape

WHAT TO DO

1. Use tracing paper to transfer the tree trunk pattern to the poster board. Make two trunks. See page 39 for the pattern.

A)

2. Paint the trunks with brown poster paint or color them with crayons or markers (See A).

3. Cut out both tree trunks (See B). On one trunk, cut a slit halfway from the top to the bottom. On the other, cut a slit halfway from the bottom to the top.

B)

c)

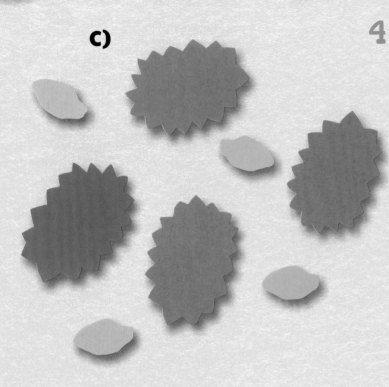

4. Use tracing paper and a pencil to transfer the leaf pattern to the green paper and the fruit patterns to any color of construction paper. See pages 40 and 42 for the patterns. Make about twenty leaves and twelve fruits. Cut them out (See C).

5. Glue the leaves to the branches of the tree. Glue leaves on both sides of the branches. Let dry. Glue the fruit on the leaves as you wish. Let dry.

6. Put the trunks together by slipping the slit on the bottom of the one trunk into the slit on the top of the other trunk (See D). Put clear tape along the line where the trunks meet.

D)

KWANZAA WORDS

Nguzo Saba are the Seven Guiding Principles that are taught at Kwanzaa. These are character traits that will help each person and his or her family accomplish great things.

Each principle has a colored candle on the kinara. The principles and their candle colors are:

1. *Umoja*—Unity (black)
2. *Kujichagulia*—Self-determination (red)
3. *Ujima*—Helping Others (green)
4. *Ujamaa*—Community Prosperity (red)
5. *Nia*—Purpose (green)
6. *Kuumba*—Creativity (red)
7. *Imani*—Faith (green)

WHAT YOU WILL NEED

- tracing paper
- pencil
- poster board or construction paper (red, green, and black)
- markers or crayons
- scissors

1. Use tracing paper and a pencil to transfer the patterns from pages 42–43 to the poster board or construction paper.

2. Decorate the letters of the words with markers or crayons.

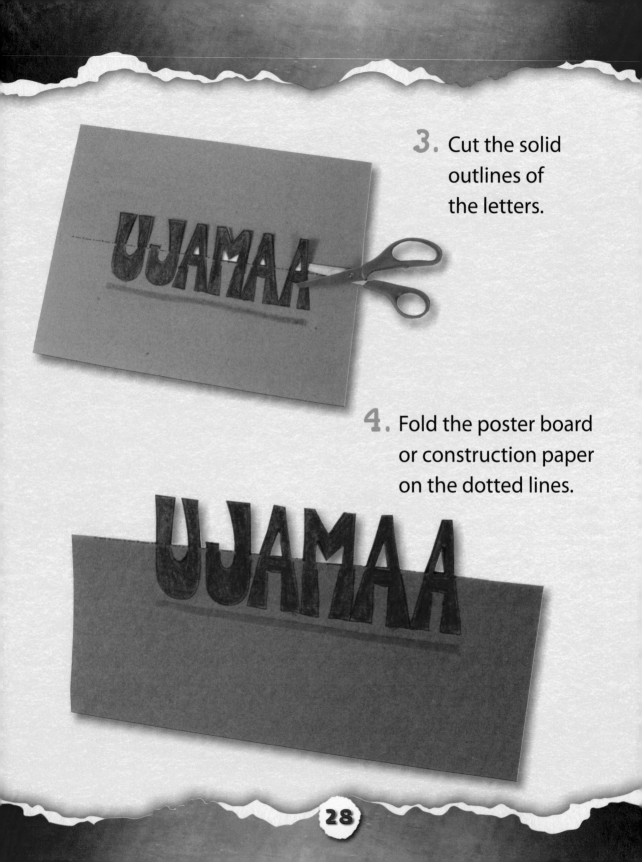

3. Cut the solid outlines of the letters.

4. Fold the poster board or construction paper on the dotted lines.

LION

The lion is one of the best known animals of Africa. Many see it as a symbol of pride and strength. Several African countries feature a lion in their national coat of arms, a design or symbol that stands for the country, like the bald eagle appears on many symbols for the United States of America. Lions are the only big cats that live and work together in groups. Though the male lions are bigger, female lions do most of the hunting. This lion decoration can represent the land of Africa at your Kwanzaa celebration.

WHAT YOU WILL NEED

- tracing paper
- pencil
- white card stock paper or poster board
- markers or crayons
- scissors
- white glue

WHAT TO DO

1. Use tracing paper and a pencil to transfer the pattern from page 40 to the card stock or poster board.

2. Color the lion and his mane. Add features to its face, such as eyes, a nose, and a mouth.

3. Cut out the lion pattern. Cut the lines along the lion's mane.

4. Fold along the dotted lines. On page 40 there is an explanation of the different types of folds.

5. Put a drop of glue on the inside of the lion's neck to hold the head in place.

6. Curl the lion's mane using your fingers.

AFRICAN-STYLE HAT

Zawadi are useful gifts that family members give one another at Kwanzaa. Zawadi are often handmade, which shows *kuumba*, or creativity. Zawadi can be items of clothing, jewelry, handbags, wallets, bookmarks, or just about anything that a person could use. Make the hat shown here to give as a gift or to wear at your Kwanzaa party.

WHAT YOU WILL NEED

- scissors
- poster board
- markers or crayons
- construction paper of any color (optional)
- pieces of cloth of any color (optional)
- masking tape
- clear tape
- tissue paper of any color

WHAT TO DO

1. Cut the poster board into strips 3 inches wide and about 24 inches long

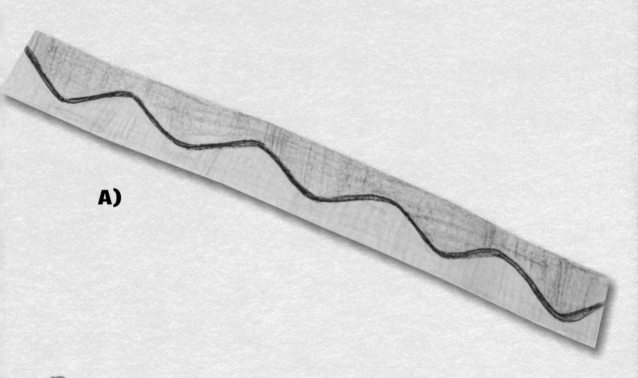

A)

2. Decorate the poster-board strips with markers, crayons, colored paper, or pieces of cloth (See A).

3. Have an adult help you wrap the strip around your head so that it fits comfortably. Use two or three pieces of masking tape on the inside of the strip to hold it together

B)

(See B). Use clear tape to hold down the loose edge on the outside of the strip. The strip is now a headband.

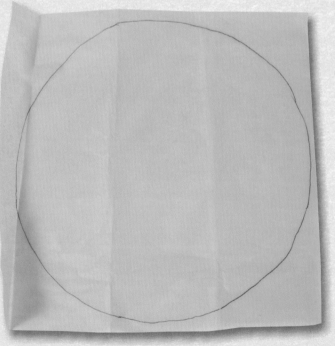

4. Cut a circle from the tissue paper that is bigger than the headband by about 2 inches all around (See C).

C)

5. Use masking tape to fasten the tissue paper to the inside edge of the headband. You will need to crimp (pinch together) the tissue paper in places to make it fit.

PATTERNS

Use tracing paper to copy the patterns on these pages.
Ask an adult to help you cut and trace the shapes.

Kinara Pop-Up Card

Cut on the solid lines.

Fold on the dotted lines.

Enlarge to 130%

Ear of Corn (Muhindi)

Enlarge to 185%

Standing Fruit Tree

The red line is where you cut on one trunk.

The green line is where you cut on the other trunk.

Enlarge to 160%

Lion

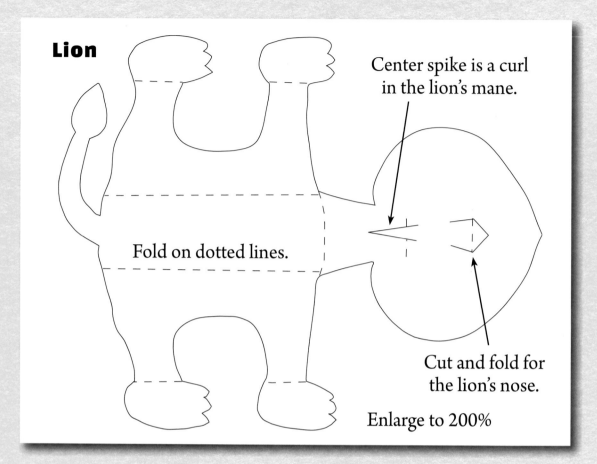

Center spike is a curl in the lion's mane.

Fold on dotted lines.

Cut and fold for the lion's nose.

Enlarge to 200%

Leaf Pattern

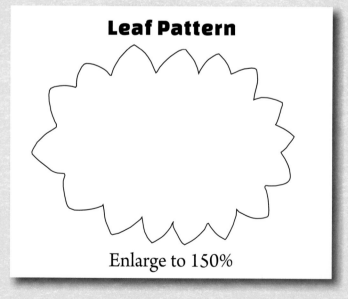

Enlarge to 150%

Flame Pattern

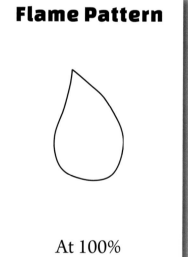

At 100%

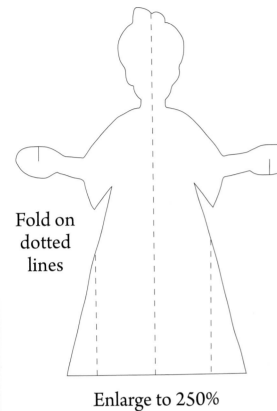

Standing
Kwanzaa Figures

Fold on
dotted
lines

Enlarge to 250%

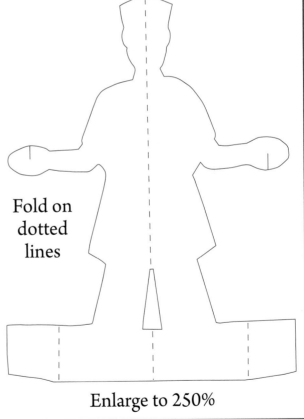

Standing
Kwanzaa Figures

Fold on
dotted
lines

Enlarge to 250%

Fruit Pattern

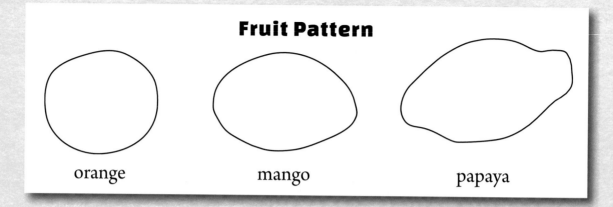

orange   mango   papaya

Kwanzaa Words

IMANI

Cut the bold black lines.

Enlarge to 200%

Fold on the dotted line.

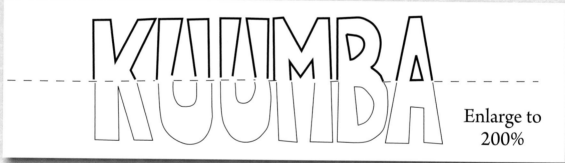

KUUMBA

Enlarge to 200%

NIA

Enlarge to 185%

KUJICHAGULIA

Enlarge to 170%

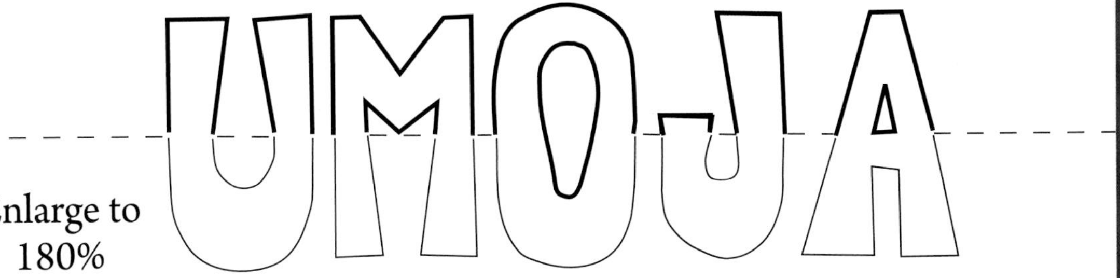

UMOJA

Enlarge to
180%

UJAMAA

Enlarge to
180%

UJIMA

Enlarge to
175%

READ ABOUT

Medearis, Angela Shelf. *Seven Spools of Thread: A Kwanzaa Story*. Morton Grove, Ill.: Albert Whitman, 2000.

Murray, Julie. *Kwanzaa*. Edina, Minn.: ABDO Pub. Co., 2003.

Nobleman, Marc Tyler. *Kwanzaa*. Minneapolis, Minn.: Compass Point Books, 2005.

Schaefer, Lola M. *Kwanzaa*. Mankato, Minn.: Pebble Books, 2001.

Winne, Joanne. *Let's Get Ready for Kwanzaa*. New York: Children's Press, 2001.

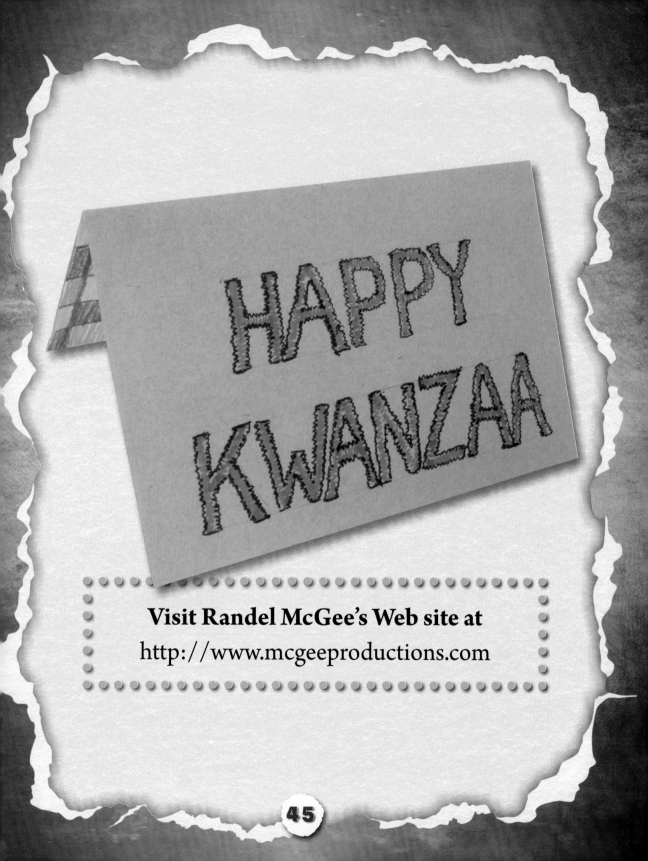

Visit Randel McGee's Web site at
http://www.mcgeeproductions.com

INDEX

ABOUT THE AUTHOR

Randel McGee has been playing with paper and scissors for as long as he can remember. As soon as he was able to get a library card, he would go to the library and find the books that showed paper crafts, check them out, take them home, and try almost every craft in the book. He still checks out books on paper crafts at the library, but he also buys books to add to his own library and researches paper-craft sites on the Internet.

McGee says, "I begin by making copies of simple crafts or designs I see in books. Once I get the idea of how something is made, I begin to make changes to make the designs more personal. After a lot of trial and error, I find ways to do something new and different that is all my own. That's when the fun begins!"

McGee also liked singing and acting from a young age. He graduated college with a degree in children's theater and specialized in puppetry. After college, he taught himself ventriloquism and started performing at libraries and schools with a friendly dragon puppet named Groark.

"Randel McGee and Groark" have toured throughout the United States and Asia, sharing their fun shows with young and old alike. Groark is the star of two award-winning video series for elementary school students on character education: *Getting Along with Groark* and *The Six Pillars of Character*.

In the 1990s, McGee combined his love of making things with paper with his love of telling stories. He tells stories while making pictures cut from paper to illustrate the tales he tells. The famous author Hans Christian Andersen also made cut-paper pictures when he told stories. McGee portrays Andersen in storytelling performances around the world.

Besides performing and making things, McGee, with the help of his wife, Marsha, likes showing librarians, teachers, fellow artists, and children the fun and educational experiences they can have with paper crafts, storytelling, drama, and puppetry. Randel McGee has belonged to the Guild of American Papercutters, the National Storytelling Network, and the International Ventriloquists' Association. He has been a regional director for the Puppeteers of America, Inc., and past president of UNIMA-USA, an international puppetry organization. He has been active in working with children and scouts in his community and church for many years. He and his wife live in California. They are the parents of five grown children who are all talented artists and performers.